The
Transcendental
Mirage

The Transcendental Mirage

by James Bjornstad

DIMENSION BOOKS
BETHANY FELLOWSHIP, INC.
Minneapolis, Minnesota

The Transcendental Mirage
by James Bjornstad

Library of Congress Catalog Card Number 76-6614

ISBN 0-87123-556-0

Copyright © 1976
Bethany Fellowship, Inc.
All Rights Reserved

DIMENSION BOOKS
Published by Bethany Fellowship, Inc.
6820 Auto Club Road, Minneapolis, Minnesota
55438

Printed in the United States of America

DEDICATED

to

Rev. Donald A. Jensen,
Pastor of Village Baptist Church
in Beaverton, Oregon, whose continual prodding
and encouragement to get my research and
thoughts on contemporary issues in writing has
brought forth this effort on Transcendental
Meditation.

ABOUT THE AUTHOR

JAMES BJORNSTAD is the founder and executive director of the Institute of Contemporary Christianity in Oakland, New Jersey. The institute is a research organization designed to analyze current issues and trends and provide answers to these from a biblical perspective. Mr. Bjornstad is also instructor in philosophy and theology at Northeastern Bible College, Essex Falls, New Jersey.

His academic credentials are very impressive. He is a member of several educational and professional societies and is included in *Who's Who in Contemporary Authors*, *Who's Who in the East*, *Who's Who in Religion*, and the *International Dictionary of Biography*.

Bjornstad graduated from Northeastern Bible College and New York Theological Seminary, and completed his thesis for a Ph.D. degree at New York University.

He has lectured extensively in public schools and universities as well as in churches and conferences throughout the nation.

He is the author of *Twentieth Century Prophecy* and *Stars, Signs, and Salvation in the Age of Aquarius*, and has written numerous articles for newspapers, magazines and journals on various contemporary issues.

PREFACE

It was in the year 1966 that I first began to notice the influence of Maharishi Mahesh Yogi and his teachings upon the Western world. The communication media here in America had just brought his message of peace and his system of transcendental meditation to the forefront as the answer to the problems of the world and mankind. Of course back then TM was more closely associated with Hinduism and better understood to be a religious practice than it is today, although it was in the very beginning of its metamorphosis from the religious to the secular.

Anticipating that it would make inroads into America, I pursued the subject by reading their materials and talking with their personnel, attempting to provide an analysis of it. The result of this was a short article entitled "Maharishi and Meditation," which was published in 1968. In it I pointed out that "this technique of 'transcendental meditation,' is really the ancient

Hindu art of meditation, refined to suit the needs of modern man in the modern situation in which man finds himself." I even pointed out some of the inherent shortcomings in the practice of TM.

Since that time I have continued in my research of this practice. Many meditators and TM instructors have been interviewed. Many lectures have been given on TM in universities, community groups, churches and conferences. The question period at the end of the lectures have been most productive in refining my thinking on this subject and defending it.

This volume reflects the conclusion of my research and thinking on TM from almost a ten-year study of it, not as a participant or meditator, but as a researcher. I do wish to express my thanks to those who have been interviewed, to those who have sat and talked with me about TM, and to those who have asked questions and even presented challenges — whether in agreement or disagreement. It has all had a part in this book.

That this book will be helpful in enlightening many as to what transcendental meditation is all about, its differences from the Gospel of Jesus Christ, and to the greatness of the life Jesus Christ offers — far superior to TM — is my sincerest prayer.

James Bjornstad

Contents

Contents

Introduction

Transcendental Meditation is sweeping across America today. TM advocates have developed a world plan, and progress is being made in its implementation as thousands follow this method of meditation.

The claims of TM are very appealing, which accounts for its amazing success all over this country. These claims listed in its publicity campaign are as follows: (1) TM is not religious. (2) TM has no metaphysical basis. (3) TM is inclusively beneficial for mankind. Each of these statements contains both explicit and implicit factors; they are made for the specific purpose of avoiding certain issues and attaining others. Thus it is important to examine these statements to see if they are true. We must note also the implications resulting from acceptance of TM. In our inquiry, we will pursue (1) The Religious Question; (2) The Metaphysical Question; and (3) The Practical Question.

The basis for such a study is found in Isaiah 41, where God challenges the religions of the world to "present their case...bring forward their strong arguments." The apostle Paul also reminds us to "test all things; hold fast to that which is good." This, too, is our concern and basis. Does TM have evidence to back its claims? Is it something good which we should hold onto?

This writer found the subject of TM quite difficult to research because of the subjectiveness of much of the data on both sides of the question. First of all, exponents of TM frequently present only the side that favors that group, utilizing parts of research to build up its case. For example, TM has used the research of Herbert Benson, Harvard Medical School, in its claim that it is unique with regard to its relaxation response. However, a letter from Dr. Benson to me denies this uniqueness; this is also shown in his new book, *The Relaxation Response*, published by William Morrow Co. Another example of TM's misuse of data and charts is demonstrated by Leon S. Otis of the Stanford Research Institute (see *Psychology Today*, April 1974, pp. 45-46). There are many other examples of TM's bias in presenting its case.

On the other side, there are those who in attempting to disprove TM also have misused the evidence. An example of this: "There is a report of a suicide rate among the meditation teachers of a nationally known discipline which is higher than the national suicide rate'' (''The Transcendental Experience: Paradise or Self Destruction,'' *The National Courier,* October 7, 1975, p. 24). In checking this report, I learned from the editor of that paper that "the discipline referred to was transcendental meditation and the report was in the form of a tape recording by a former TM teacher." (Obviously, the claim of one former TM teacher is not sufficient to prove the above published statement.)

In the analysis which follows, the evidence was examined as carefully as possible. The conclusions have been drawn from evidence which is readily available to anyone.

The
Transcendental
Mirage

I. The Religious Question

"It is not religious," claims the Maharishi Mahesh Yogi, founder and leader of the modern TM movement. This same position has been espoused and reiterated in TM's literature, as well as in lectures and public appearances by TM instructors and personnel. Even in a *Reader's Digest* article on TM (Dec. 1975), it is presented as religiously neutral. Under this guise, TM has been the recipient of both federal and state funding. It has been accepted in the curriculum of many public schools. Furthermore, it has been able to attract adherents of many of the world's religions, including Christianity, to its practice.

If TM is shown to have religious aspects, there would be great difficulties with the above. Would TM advocates be telling the "whole truth" in their advertising? Should they receive federal and state funding for programs? What about the doctrine of the separation of Church and State? How could a student in a public school be required to participate in it? How could a religious person participate in it, especially if it was in direct opposition to his or her faith? There are many other questions and implications which could be pursued. Certainly the religious question is an important one, worthy of our utmost concern and most careful scrutiny.

Students of Comparative Religions have had no difficulty in understanding TM as religious. They recognize it as an aspect of ancient Indian Brahmanism and Hinduism, that its origins lie in the ancient texts of Hinduism — The *Vedas, Upanishads* and the *Bhagavad-Gita* — and that its development came about through Shankara's synthesis of these traditions. They know that it grew out of the mystical Advaita school of Yoga, and that it used the Hindu devotional — a puja — as an initiation ritual. This has been the historic understanding of TM.

Interestingly, exactly the same basis for origin and development is set forth by TM's founder, Maharishi Mahesh Yogi, and by one of its leading instructors, Jack Forem. According to them the origin of TM was through Lord Krishna who gave this teaching or technique to the warrior Arjuna some 5000 years ago. (The account of this can be found in the *Bhagavad-Gita.*) Notice: *this technique of TM was given to a man by a Hindu deity.* Within 2000 years its practice was lost through lack of usage. Buddha restored this concept of Being, according to TM, but shortly thereafter it was lost again. Then about 2500 years ago Shankara, a great teacher and commentator on the sacred Hindu scriptures, revived it again. After a period of time the teaching was lost for the third time in its history. In our generation the Maharishi's teacher, Brahmanand Saraswati Maharaj (better known as Shri Guru Dev), revived this teaching in Hinduism. Shri Guru Dev was born in 1869; he died in 1953. He passed this teaching on to his favorite pupil, the Maharishi Mahesh Yogi.[1] So, TM has been perpetuated through the years in Hinduism as a sect of that religion. It is clear that we are in the third revival of this aspect in Hinduism, and that this wave of revival has now come out of India and the East into the West.

TM does acknowledge its Hindu heritage. *But* its followers deny that it is Hindu or religious today. It is extremely difficult, if not impossible, to understand this line of reasoning. Several possible answers to this enigma have been suggested — some by TM instructors and some by non-TM investigators. Only one, though, seems to fit all of the details involved in this puzzle.

The Maharishi left his secluded life as a Hindu monk in the Himalayas in 1958 to bring his message of peace and his teaching of Transcendental Meditation to the West. At this time the movement was known as the Spiritual

Regeneration Movement. The Maharishi came to England with his message but was not accepted. In fact, 100 copies of a book about the Maharishi were imported and only 60 were sold. It was not until 1966 that some (the Beatles, Mia Farrow, and others) began to take notice of him and to meditate. But even then there was no massive turning to TM. The facts indicate that the great interest and increase in TM and meditating came *only after* the Maharishi changed his way of relating his teaching to the world. In other words, when he made it applicable to the Western world. The Maharishi stated this when he wrote: "Not in the name of God-realization can we call a man to meditate in the world today, but in the name of enjoying the world better, sleeping well at night, being wide awake during the day." [2] Of course, simply *presenting it in a different light does not change the essence of TM; it is still Hinduism.* Though a chameleon changes color to blend with its surroundings, it remains a chameleon at all times. But, there is still much more evidence to consider.

What exactly is meant by "religion"? Philosophically, attempts to define this term or category have generally been unsuccessful in gaining universal agreement. And yet all definitions seem to share two common elements: awareness of the Transcendent ("superior or supreme"), and man's approach to the Transcendent. Obviously, the very descriptor *Transcendental* reveals awareness of the Transcendent, and *Meditation* refers to the way one can approach, contact and experience the Transcendent. Thus Transcendental Meditation is man's approach (through the mantra) to the Transcendent (attaining God Consciousness). Philosophically, TM includes the two main elements found in all definitions of religion.

To go beyond the essentials mentioned above, we should include several other aspects. These aspects can be noted in various dictionary definitions of the term "religion." Consider the following:

> The service and adoration of God or a God as expressed in forms of worship, in obedience to divine commands, especially as found in accepted sacred writings or as declared by recognized teachers and in a pursuit of a way of life incumbent on true believers....[3]

Included in the above definition are the following categories: (1) service and adoration of God; (2) forms of worship; (3) sacred writings; (4) recognized teachers; and (5) the only true way of life. Can we find all of these aspects in TM? If we can, then TM should be categorized or classified as religious.

In our examination we will look to the practices and literature of TM, especially the less widely publicized yet authoritative writings of the founder and leader of the entire movement today, the Maharishi Mahesh Yogi.

The first of the categories is that of *service and adoration of God.* Religion includes service and adoration, although varying widely as to how this is done and even more widely as to the concept of "God." TM also has service and adoration, although in the broader sense, for it must be understood in its Hindu framework as to how man serves and adores that concept of God as Brahman.

No one can read any of the available writings of the Maharishi without noting his continuous references to God. However, the Maharishi's God is not a personal Lord of the universe but rather the impersonal Brahman of Hinduism.[4] As Anthony Campbell has noted: "Maharishi is not talking about God as an object of belief or even primarily of worship; he is saying that to someone whose awareness has revealed this state (i.e., God Consciousness), the world is 'glorified' and takes on a personal quality."[5] So it is the Hindu concept of an impersonal God that the Maharishi is promoting for our service and adoration. Says the Maharishi, "Surrender to the almighty will of God...is possible *only* in the state of transcendental consciousness which is easily arrived at by the simple system of transcendental deep meditation."[6] To go further, the one who regularly practices TM "is in the hands of God for the purpose of God."[7] When one practices TM one is serving and adoring Brahman, doing its will and serving it.

Secondly, as religion has its *forms of worship,* its rites and rituals, so it is with TM. After the first two introductory lectures on TM, if one is still determined to meditate "Maharishi style," one could do so only by joining the movement. One must first have an interview with an instructor and pay an initiation fee. Then comes the moment of joining — the initiation ceremony.

Like Hindus following the tradition of Shankara, one must bring offerings of six flowers, three pieces of fruit, and a white handkerchief. Evidently the flowers are representative of life; the fruit, the seed of life; and the handkerchief, the cleansing of the spirit. (Hindus do not offer animals as sacrifices or offerings because of their belief in reincarnation — it might be a relative.) First one removes his shoes (like entering into a holy place) and is led into a small room illumined by candlelight and permeated with incense. There is a table holding a picture of the Maharishi's teacher, Shri Guru Dev. This is a "mirti," a form made manifest for his worshippers. The initiate is placed before an altar and the teacher begins to sing the Puja, a Vedic hymn of worship acknowledging the departed masters (deities) of the Shankara tradition of Hinduism. As the instructor acknowledges these masters, he bows and makes his offering. In fact, the picture of the Shri Guru Dev becomes focal, for he is worshipped as the incarnation of the Hindu Trinity. (See the translation of the entire Puja in Appendix A in the back of this book.) When this ceremony is completed, the initiate receives his mantra, his secret Sanskrit sound to be used in his meditating.

Instructors in TM maintain that this ceremony is not religious. They have explained that this ceremony is only "Indian hospitality." You know, "When in Rome, do what the Romans do." Jhan Robbins and David Fisher have explained it with a slightly different twist: "...the fruit, flowers and handkerchief have no practical use. They are a traditional part of the ceremony, and are to TM what white wigs are to English barristers." [8] Analogies are nice to use, but the atmosphere of this ceremony is not in the class of both "Indian hospitality" and "English barristers."

Many who go through the ceremony have difficulty ignoring the religious aspects that their instructors attempt to gloss over. Penelope McMillan writes: "It's not supposed to be a religious ceremony, but the teacher moves things around the altar like he's celebrating some kind of high mass." [9]

Furthermore, the Maharishi doesn't try to hide the meanings of the rituals or pass them off as hospitality. Says the Maharishi: "All that we do, we make our offerings to our master...offer a flower...offering of handkerchief...all these rites and rituals...supplement...the mantras.... This has a very, very great meaning."[10] In fact the Maharishi also sees worship involved in this ceremony: "The Holy Tradition of great masters which is responsible for reviving this teaching after every lapse...is not merely to be held in high regard, but has come to be actually *worshipped* by seekers of Truth and knowers of Reality."[11] The Maharishi readily admits that this ceremony involves rites and rituals — forms of worship.

If one refuses to bring the offering or totally objects to the Puja and the ceremony, he will not be initiated and allowed to join. In other words, TM is an exclusive group, a closed religious movement. In order to become a member one must come with offerings to the deities and also participate (even if passively) in the worship of, and be presented to, the gods of this Hindu sect. At the conclusion of this ceremony one becomes a member. Is this not comparable to joining a church or any religious movement? Certainly these are forms of worship.

Thirdly, as religion includes *sacred writings* or scriptures, so does TM. TM is set forth only in the Hindu scriptures as translated by their teacher, the Maharishi Mahesh Yogi, and these scriptures become the basis for the entire movement. David Bolling noted this "heart" of the nerve center at the Maharishi International University. "The Vedic Studies Room exudes an air of sober scholarship. Bookshelves are lined with Vedic texts, translations of the *Bhagavad-Gita,* the *Brahma Sutras* and the *Upanishads*.... Foremost among the Vedic studies being pursued is a unique commentary on the *Rig Veda*.... In addition...a commentary on the *Brahma Sutras* is 75% finished, and future plans include more commentary on the *Bhagavad-Gita*...."[12] In other words, the entire movement is wrapped up in understanding the Hindu scriptures.

TM is set forth both in origin and technique in the *Bhagavad-Gita.* Says the Maharishi, "The *Bhagavad-Gita* is the Light of Life, lit by God at the altar of man to save humanity from the darkness of ignorance and suffering...."[13] "The *Bhagavad-Gita* gives a very clear exposition of the path of enlightenment, the transcendental deep meditation."[14] Of note is the fact that TM is found *only* in the Hindu scriptures, explicitly, in the *Bhagavad-Gita* — and, more explicitly, *only* in the Maharishi's translation and commentary of those scriptures. It is not found in the scriptures of the other religions of the world.

Fourthly, ordained, appointed or *recognized teachers* who not only "preach" or demonstrate its message but also care for its members is a part of the category which constitutes religion. This area can also be found in TM. The Mararishi says: "One learns about the nature of the world and reality from a teacher...." [15] Furthermore, "the practice of transcendental deep meditation must always be given by the expert masters of meditation who have been properly trained to give it and who have been trained to check its experience." [16] As churches and various religious movements have their pastors, clergy and holy men, so TM has its teachers.

Each teacher is a "holy man," having received his training from his teacher, the Maharishi Mahesh Yogi, and each signs a contract with him which concludes with the statement: "...I have been accepted to serve the Holy Tradition and spread the light of God to all those who need it...."

Fifthly, religion includes the claim that it has the way to God or the Ultimate and the way to life. This way of life is incumbent on the true believer. This aspect of religion can also be seen in TM. The Maharishi says that TM is "the *only way* out of the field of sin," [17] and that it is "the *only way* to salvation and success in life; there is no other way." [18] Can it be any clearer that TM believers feel they have the *only* true way and that all other movements, groups and practices do not have the truth and the way to life? As such, it is incumbent on every *true* believer to make converts.

Certainly TM contains all of the elements which comprise the above popular definition of religion. TM should be classified in that category — as religious. But whatever definition of religion one chooses, TM will be found to meet the requirements necessary to be classified as such.

From a legal viewpoint, Supreme Court Justice William O. Douglas has provided us with a concise statement of Hinduism — the same basis as the Maharishi sets forth in his writings —as Religion. (See *United States v. Seeger,* 380 U.S. 163 (1965).)

There is one other way, a completely different approach to this entire question which we need to examine. TM advocates claim that it is not religious. What definition of religion do they use which excludes them? What is it that TM is not?

The Maharishi gives us his definition of the term religion: " 'Religion' comes from the Latin root 'religire,' meaning 're,' back; 'ligire,' to bind; or, that which binds one back. The purpose of religion is to bind man back to his source, his origin." [19] However, TM does claim to be the only way of binding one back to that from which he came, to Brahman, the alleged Hindu source of all existence and thought. [20] Therefore, TM is religious on the basis of the Maharishi's own definition.

Once one understands something of the Eastern way of thinking about the world and everything which exists, then the fact of TM as a religion becomes quite clear. Whether one accepts the judgment of students of the world's religions or if one examines what constitutes the classification of religion philosophically, by popular definition or by the Maharishi's definition, one cannot escape the conclusion from the evidence that TM is a sect of Hinduism. It is religious.

Notes

1. *Maharishi Mahesh Yogi on the Bhagavad-Gita*, pp. 10-16, and Jack Forem, *Transcendental Meditation*, pp. 293-294.
2. *Meditations of the Maharishi Mahesh Yogi*, p. 168.
3. *Webster's New International Dictionary*.
4. *E.g.*, Maharishi Mahesh Yogi, *Transcendental Meditation: Serenity Without Drugs*, p. 33, and *Maharishi Mahesh Yogi on the Bhagavad-Gita*.
5. Anthony Campbell, *Seven States of Consciousness: A Vision of Possibility Suggested by the Teachings of Maharishi Mahesh Yogi*, p. 94.
6. *Transcendental Meditation: Serenity Without Drugs*, p. 96.
7. *Ibid.*, p. 97.
8. Jhan Robbins and David Fisher, *Tranquility Without Pills: All About Transcendental Meditation*, p. 43.
9. Penelope McMillan, "The Hard Sell Comes To Meditation," *New York Sunday News*, November 2, 1975, p. 10.
10. *Meditations of the Maharishi Mahesh Yogi*, p. 39.
11. *Maharishi Mahesh Yogi on the Bhagavad-Gita*, p. 257.
12. David Bolling, *MIU International Newsletter*, Vol. I, No. 1, February 1972, pp. 9-10.
13. *Maharishi Mahesh Yogi on the Bhagavad-Gita*, pp. 19-20.

14. *Transcendental Meditation: Serenity Without Drugs,* p. 34.

15. *Ibid.,* p. 270.

16. *Ibid.,* p. 52.

17. *Maharishi Mahesh Yogi on the Bhagavad-Gita,* p. 207.

18. *Ibid.,* p. 228.

19. *Transcendental Meditation: Serenity Without Drugs,* pp. 249-250.

20. *E.g., Transcendental Meditation: Serenity Without Drugs,* and *Maharishi Mahesh Yogi on the Bhagavad-Gita* as to the basic understanding of Being from which everything had its origin, and man's quest for Being or return to the source.

II. The Metaphysical Question

Metaphysics is the branch of philosophy which deals with the ultimate nature of existence, reality, experience. TM claims to have no metaphysical basis; it is merely a technique which can be used in any system, religion or philosophy. Whether one is Christian, Muslim, Jewish, Hindu or Atheist, all can meditate. Is this claim really true?

Is there a common characteristic, doctrine, religion or technique by which all of the metaphysical systems — religious and philosophical — can be identified or compared? Many have thought that such an area existed, and before the modern era they sought this common basis in some doctrine. Within this century other bases of comparison have been sought, such as the affirmation or denial of the reality of existence, or the handling of the problem of suffering. In our day, TM is said to be the common basis. But the more one studies the religions of the world, the more one discovers that the characteristic most fully shared by all of the religions and philosophies of the world is their incompatibility with each other.

We have already noted that TM is a sect or branch of Hinduism. At this point the least we can say is that TM functions in the Hindu metaphysical system. But can it function in *all* systems? This is the question.

In this section we will consider the metaphysical framework of TM (which is Hindu) as noted and declared by the Maharishi Mahesh Yogi in his book *Transcendental Meditation: Serenity Without Drugs*. Note his system and the system of TM carefully. It is so important that the Maharishi says in his introduction: "This book is divided into four sections: 'Science of Being'; 'Life'; 'Art of Living'; and 'Fulfillment.' The last three sections of the book...is based...in the section on the Science of Being" (p. xvi). In other words, in order to understand life and live it fully, one must understand this particular metaphysical system. Why? Because it is the one in which TM exists. It is the metaphysical system in which their doctrine of man exists and also their solution — TM.

Below is a simple layperson's understanding of TM's metaphysical system. As a Christian and a firm believer in Jesus Christ, I will compare it with Christianity's metaphysical system. Please note the distinct irreconcilable differences.

A. The Ultimate

TM — BEING

CHRISTIANITY — GOD

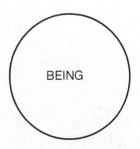

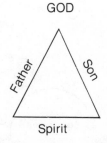

Being is commonly called God, the Supreme Lord of the Universe and Brahman.[1] Being is impersonal, nonchanging, formless and eternal,[2] the source of everything and from which everything evolved. It is described as omnipotent, omniscient and omnipresent.[3] Being underlies and encompasses all that exists.[4]

God is Personal Infinite Spirit, eternal and complete in himself. God is one, yet eternally exists as three persons — Father, Son and Holy Spirit; one unity (Triunity) in which love, fellowship, communication and interpersonal relations exist always.

B. The World

TM — EMANATES
FROM BEING

CHRISTIANITY —
CREATED OUT OF
NOTHING

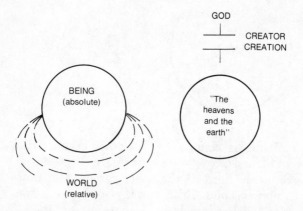

The world is not created; it eternally emanates from the divine Being. It flows out from Being and back into Being.[5] Being alone is Absolute—the Real. Emanation, or that which flows out from Being is a part of

God created the world out of nothing. It is separate and distinct from His being, and did not flow out nor emanate from His essence (Ps. 33:6; Rom. 4:17; Heb. 11:3; etc.). The world is real, it had a beginning and

Being, but yet different from Being.[6] Emanations are not the real, but the less real. Thus the world we live in is the furthest removed from Being; it is relative existence, the world of appearances, illusion or "mirage."[7]

it will have an end. God made it thus.

C. The Person

TM — EXTENSION OF BEING

CHRISTIANITY — CREATED BY GOD

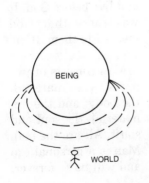

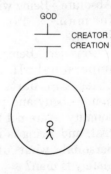

Man is an extension of Being out in the relative existence of the world. Man consists of all of the manifestations of Being from the Absolute to the Relative. Thus, man consists of three aspects: the outer, the inner and the transcendent. These correspond to body, personality and Being. Since body and personality belong to the relative existence of man, the focus of man must be upon the Absolute—Being within man.[8] Man is Divine.[9]

Consider; Being is impersonal. If the other two parts of man — body and personality — are not the real, and Being is impersonal, what ultimately is man?

Man is created in the image of God, not as a part of nor an extension of God. Man is the creature and God, the Creator. This distinction is never blurred in the Bible. Man is not divine. God, being external to creation and distinct from it, took the dust of the ground, breathed into it, giving it life, and Adam was created. Together with Eve, whom God fashioned from a part of Adam, man was placed in the Garden to care for it and live before God. It was there that God met with them (Gen. 1, 2).

Man consists of two parts: the material, the body; and the immaterial, the soul and spirit. All are the real. Man is a personal ego and will be so forever.

D. The Problem

TM —
METAPHYSICAL

CHRISTIANITY —
MORAL

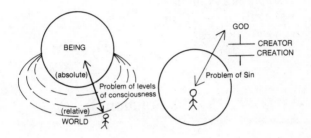

Man's problem is his metaphysical separation from Being by levels of consciousness. Man lives in the outer relative existence of Being, the world, and needs to return to the absolute existence of Being.[10] Man's deepest difficulty lies in his lack of consciousness

Man has disobeyed God's commandments and this sin has affected the entire course of human history (Gen. 3:14-19; Rom. 5:15, 17). Man's basic problem is that he is morally bankrupt in God's sight, that he has sinned and disobeyed God. Thus, his basic problem is his in-of his own divine being. He needs the key to help him evolve through each of the seven stages of consciousness to Being.[11] Man needs to be metaphysically unified with Being — God consciousness.

solence and alienation from his Creator in his heart and mind. Man needs to be reconciled to and made right with God.

E. The Solution

TM —
TRANSCENDENTAL
MEDITATION

CHRISTIANITY —
JESUS CHRIST

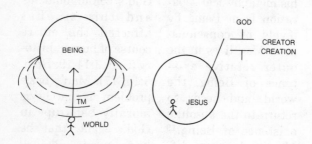

If man's problem is metaphysical in that man is estranged from Being by levels of consciousness, then the key to salvation lies in finding a way through these levels, returning to his true nature, or Being. Numerous practices and ways have been set forth for use in contacting Being. For example, the breathing exercises of Yoga are used to invoke Prana, the vibrating nature of Being.[12] Reincarnation is a way through which man can return to Being through many lifetimes.[13] All of these are mentioned by the Maharishi as true, but to him the greatest method of salvation — the *unique* way — is TM. TM lifts one from the wheel of fate and is the

If man's problem is his alienation from God because of sin, then a payment for sin is needed to be reconciled to God. Man is unable to provide this, so God himself took the initiative in history in the incarnation of Jesus Christ who was fully God and man. Jesus' death on the cross was to pay the penalty for our sins. It was predetermined that God would obtain salvation in this way and offer it as a free gift to all who would accept His Son (Rom. 5:8-11; Gal. 1:14).

Jesus' bodily resurrection from the dead guarantees that He has redeemed man totally — physically and spiritually. The believer looks forward to that day of resurrection when he only way to discover the God-self or Being in its fullness. To meditate, one uses a mantra — a sacred Sanskrit sound — to transcend the levels or consciousness[14] and to attain oneness with Being or the state of God Consciousness.[15]

shall be made complete (Rom. 8:23-24; I John 3:2,3; I Cor. 15; etc.).

Man is saved — made right before God only through surrender of his life to the risen Lord Jesus Christ as Savior. Jesus alone is the *only* way to life and to God (John 14:6). One must recognize his own condition before God as a sinner, confess his sins and trust Christ alone for acceptance with God (Gal. 2:16; Eph. 2:8-9).

Returning to our main concern in this section, can TM be a common technique or factor in all religions? Is TM the same in Hinduism as it is in the Christian framework? With such diverse understandings about the Ultimate or God, the creation which exists, man and his problem, and the solution to man's problem, can TM carry with it the same meaning and understanding across both structures, across all religions? Obviously not! The meaning and purpose of Maharishi's technique derives its basis from, and exists only in, the Hindu or a similar framework and not in the Christian framework. You see, it is the metaphysical structure, the religious framework, which interprets the technique, and not vice versa.

To clarify one area, Christianity does encourage meditation — meditation centered on God (Ps. 63:6), God's Law (Ps. 119: 15, 23, 97) and God's Works (Ps. 77:12). This is entirely different from TM — meditation "Maharishi style."

If it is true that TM is Hindu and that it operates in a Hindu metaphysical system, as we have noted, they why do its teachers continue to set forth its technique as nonmetaphysical? Perhaps because the Maharishi believes there is no other metaphysical system but his and/or that his is the true one. Therefore he interprets everything in the Hindu framework. For example, the Maharishi accepts all religions as paths to God (his concept of God). How does he do this? By transforming them into an aspect of Hinduism, in line with his theology of Being. Says the Maharishi: "It does not matter whether they call themselves Christians, Mohammedans, Hindu, or Buddhist.... On the gross level of life these names carry significance, but on the level of Being, they all have the same value." [16] In like manner the Maharishi transforms other aspects into his system and interprets them with a Hindu flavor.

On the other hand, if TM is viewed in the framework of historic biblical Christianity, different meanings, alternative interpretations are given to the TM experience. Certainly experience cannot be denied, but one can question its meaning and the interpretation given to it. This is exactly the case when one views TM from a Christian perspective.

According to the Bible there is a personal Creator God who made a real universe and all that exists distinct from himself. According to this, God's testimony, there is only one way to experience Him, and that is through an act of faith in the person and work of Jesus Christ. Therefore, because TM does not follow this divinely prescribed formula, their experience cannot be an experience of that God. Hence it must be relegated to another realm. Several alternative interpretations have been suggested as to the reality of the TM experience. Gordon R. Lewis categorizes four of them: (1) deceptive self-hypnosis; (2) simple self-deification; (3) nonredemptive natural religion; and (4) demonic deception.[17]

Which interpretation(s) of the TM experience is true, if any? What conclusion does the evidence demand?

On the basis of objective evidence, the truth of the Christian framework is supported by the fact that the biblical God acts in history (which can be verified) and by the fact that He himself entered history in the person of Jesus Christ. Jesus claimed to be God, permitted himself to be unjustifiably killed by man, and three days later rose up from the dead, validating His claims and ministry. Christianity does not appeal to subjective experiences for validity but to an empty tomb in objective history.

In like manner, the truth of the Christian interpretation of experiences, including TM, is verified by the empirical data garnered from testing as well as from the experiences themselves. In the next section we will consider this data.

There is no doubt that TM is metaphysical. It is essentially Hinduism, the theological basis of which is monism, i.e., everything is explainable in terms of the one God or Being. Since the metaphysical structure interprets and gives true meaning to one's experience, the interpretation of the TM experience in Hinduism is radically different from that in Christianity. Thus the problem narrows down to which structure is correct. If Christianity is true, then the TM experience is not what TM advocates claim. This brings us to the next question.

Notes

1. Maharishi Mahesh Yogi, *Transcendental Meditation: Serenity Without Drugs,* pp. 33-34.
2. Ibid., pp. 265-266.
3. Ibid., pp. 22, 24-25.
4. Ibid., p. 23.
5. Ibid., p. 271.
6. Ibid., pp. 61-62.
7. Ibid., pp. 276, 283.
8. Ibid., p. 63.
9. Ibid., p. 251.
10. Ibid., p. 44.
11. Ibid., p. 66.
12. Ibid., p. 105.
13. Ibid., p. 110.
14. Ibid., p. 51.
15. Ibid., p. 81.
16. Ibid., p. 254.
17. Gordon R. Lewis, *What Everyone Should Know About Transcendental Meditation,* pp. 63-67.

III. The Practical Question

"So what if it *is* religious?" you ask. "Is it good for me? Will it make me a better person?" For some, the fact that TM is an aspect of Hinduism is sufficient reason to stay away from it. But for others, the only concern is the pragmatic one, "Does it work? Is it useful? Is it good for me?"

The title of a recent *Time* magazine article "Forty Minutes To Bliss," [1] seems to say it all — at least from the TM viewpoint: the time necessary each day to practice this simple technique of transcendental meditation, as well as the state of mind resulting from such a practice. Certainly these are great claims.

Though the realities of TM have been obscured by many of its supporters, [2] there has been no lack when it comes to making exorbitant claims for it. TM has been claimed to be the cure-all for just about everything — from education to science to government to religion; from drugs to alcoholism to chain smoking; and from lack of energy to poor sexual performance. Though there are some in TM who do not see transcendental meditation as a panacea for all the ills of mankind,[3] many TM instructors as well the International Meditation Society do. They make fantastic claims as to the benefits of transcendental meditation.

The General Assembly of the House of Representatives in the State of Illinois passed resolution No. 677 on May 24, 1972, which exemplifies some of the broad sweeping generalizations made by TM:

(1) To develop the full potential of the individual.

(2) To improve governmental achievements.

(3) To realize the highest ideal of education.

(4) To solve the problems of crime, drug abuse, and all behavior that brings unhappiness to the family of man.

(5) To maximize the intelligent use of environment.

(6) To bring fulfillment to the economic aspirations of individuals and society.

(7) To achieve the spiritual goals of mankind in this generation.

The above goals were not merely developed by some congressman as he perceives transcendental meditation, but they actually are the seven goals of the World Plan of TM.[4]

Just how great is transcendental meditation? Does it really provide all of the benefits it claims to produce? Is it unique? To these questions many answer YES! And the basis for such a reply lies in the case histories and testimonies of people who have been helped by TM, as well as in scientific research. Let's consider this basis to see if such a conclusion is warranted.

First of all, transcendental meditation points to the many who have tried it and found it helpful. No one can deny that it has helped some. For example, a Roman Catholic priest and director of a high school in his Diocese says, "I have found it effective as a means to prepare myself for the day's activity, and find that after meditating in the afternoon I no longer carry the tiredness from the day's work through to my evening's engagement." [5] A director of guidance in a New Jersey school says, "We find that the kids who started meditation seemed less uptight." [6] An army general who works in the Pentagon says, "I find it relaxing and invigorating, but I find it difficult to find the time for it." [7]

But there are also those who demonstrate the ineffectiveness of transcendental meditation. For example, a housewife practicing TM says: "I don't see a bit of difference in my life, and it's a nuisance. I'll try it a little longer; then I'm quitting." [8] A student who had tried transcendental meditation appeared before a school board to say that he did not see any practical benefits to be gained by students practicing TM. [9] A beauty parlor operator says, "Look, I really tried it. I paid my $125, attended all the sessions, and sub-

mitted to a ridiculous initiation ceremony. I
meditated for 6 months, and do you know what
happened? I fell asleep every time...." [10] In fact,
TM officials have estimated that about 20-25%
of those who start transcendental meditation
give it up after a while. [11] Though there are many
different reasons for these having stopped
meditating, at least some found that it did ab-
solutely nothing for them.

What do the case histories and testimonies of
those who practiced transcendental meditation
prove? TM has worked for some and not for
others. Dr. Leon S. Otis of Stanford Research Institute concludes similarly from his investiga-
tion: "After a series of experiments, I have come
to the conclusion that TM can probably benefit a
large number of Americans. For many others I
think it will turn out to be a waste of time. [12]

In this light, Jhan Robbins and David Fisher
relate a humorous account:

> Last season, the exasperated manager of a
> semipro baseball team watched his club drop
> seven games in a row. He tried frantically to
> reverse the losing streak with rabbits' feet and
> four-leaf clovers. Nothing worked. Finally, in
> desperation, he took the advice of his wife, a
> meditator, and had a teacher of TM instruct
> his players in the method. After the final lec-
> ture the members of the now happily meditat-
> ing team announced resolutely that they were
> ready for all opponents. They lost their remain-
> ing four games, finishing securely in last
> place. [13]

In addition to the fact that in many cases transcendental meditation provided no added benefit, there are also a few cases in which it proved to be harmful. For example, Dr. Herbert Benson of Harvard Medical School provided the research for TM regarding cases of severe migrane headaches. Out of seventeen cases studied, three were helped by meditating, thirteen showed no significant change, but one "was actually made worse."[14] In a small test using TM, Dr. Otis discovered that some psychosomatic reactions previously under control surface during meditation in a few patients.[15]

Secondly, Transcendental Meditation points to scientific data in support of its greatness and uniqueness. The verification of science is important to TM. As Paul H. Levine states: "The anecdotal claims for TM, even when they are echoed by people of unquestioned objectivity and stature, must nevertheless be verified by the tools of science before they can be accepted by a society grappling with the very ills TM is purported to relieve so effortlessly."[16] But it should be noted that much of the research on transcendental meditation has been carried on under the auspices of the TM organization or has been published by the Maharishi International University Press. And of course it is all favorable to their position. From this TM has concluded that "scientific research has verified that these are truly the fundamentals of progress that will improve the quality of life by allowing everyone to develop his full potential of mind and body and thereby to spontaneously contribute his maximum to progress and enjoy fulfillment in life."[17]

Yet many scholars, doctors and scientists do not believe that the tests available thus far are sufficient to demonstrate the superiority of transcendental meditation. For example, commenting on the drug studies regarding TM, Dr. Una Kroll says, "Nearly all the reported projects at present suffer from being too small and inadequately controlled."[18] In fact, Dr. Benson, who did the initial studies on TM's effect upon drugs, says the same thing regarding his studies.[19] In summing up the present studies in all areas, Gary Schwartz perhaps states the consensus of many when he concluded: "We should remain wary of the claims and selective use of scientific data by well-meaning but scientifically unsophisticated practitioners."[20]

Furthermore, current studies do not demonstrate the claims of Transcendental Meditation's uniqueness, thus detracting from its greatness. It is not the only technique to bring about the relaxation response. Dr. Benson, whose research gave Transcendental Meditation much of its credibility, points out that "as the experiments progressed over several years the concept developed that the various physiologic changes that accompanied Transcendental Meditation...were in no way unique to Transcendental

Meditation."[21] Since Dr. Benson's research has been used by TM in its support, it is only fair that the whole of Dr. Benson's findings be stated and accepted. At present, TM is not happy with him because of his book *The Relaxation Response,* in which he points out the results of his research in TM and the nonuniqueness of transcendental meditation. He also points out alternatives to TM which produce the same relaxation response.

There are others also who do not see the uniqueness nor greatness of TM, such as Dr. Laragh, director of the Cardio Vascular Unit at New York's Cornell Medical Center, who sees TM about as unique for relaxing as sitting on a couch or reading a book.[22]

Whether one considers testimonies of transcendental meditators or the scientific evidence in controlled experimentation, on the basis of the evidence in hand one must conclude that the claims of greatness and uniqueness are not justified. The evidence simply does not deserve this conclusion.

Another major question to consider is whether or not there are any dangers involved in practicing transcendental meditation. As one quite knowledgeable in mysticism and meditation points out, "If travel in outer space is fraught with danger, in such wise that we need intrepid astronauts, even more perilous is the inner journey into the caverns of the mind."[23]

There seems to be little or no concern on the part of TM officials or instructors about any problems or dangers inherent in the practice of transcendental meditation. It is never once mentioned in any of their public literature. Some instructors have told this researcher that some "thoughts" have surfaced, but that they merely told the initiate to "forget that thought" or "lay it aside." Dr. Kroll raises the question before us when in a forum with some TM leaders she stated, "I am puzzled by your ignoring the journey." [24]

Let's consider a few of the problems or danger areas which one might encounter while meditating TM style. First of all, there can be dangers involved in producing altered states of consciousness. These could, in extreme cases, lead even to attempts of suicide.[25] Dr. Kroll states, "If you alter the state of the automatic nervous system, you alter the level of hormones in the hypothalamic part of the brain. This is where I see possible dangers." [26]

Secondly, it could lead to psychological problems. Dr. Otis points out that the technique of "self-paced desensitization," as he refers to TM, could lead if uncontrolled to "the release of massive uncontrolled anxiety." [27] Dr. Kroll reminded TM leaders that as people meditate within themselves, as they become more aware, they could "run into things — obsessions, rages — which have been buried. They can become

aware of daemonic forces within themselves."[28]
It is possible that meditation, as Barbara Brown
has stated, "can produce the sensation of separation from the material universe, a depersonalization, loss of individual identity, and an awareness of the unifying thread of life."[29] If the
Maharishi's metaphysical system, as noted in
the last chapter, is what TM is all about, then
one should expect some of these noted problems
in a system that affirms neither one's personality
nor the world as actually the Real.

Thirdly, transcendental meditation can lead
to dangers with demons. The following account
demonstrates this problem and the fact that
some, while meditating, have experienced such a
danger.

> As my consciousness extended, I became
> aware of the presence of spirit beings sitting on
> either side of me when I was meditating, and
> sometimes, at night, they would sit on my bed. I
> spent three months meditating from three to
> ten hours a day. I had vivid experiences of
> demonic oppression while there. I awoke with a
> sense of fear and apprehension as pressure was
> being put all over my head and body by a spirit
> who was trying to enter my body.[30]

This researcher has also had the opportunity to
work with and counsel several who have experienced similar things in their meditating.

That spirits can be contacted in the process of
meditation should come as no surprise, since

even the Maharishi Mahesh Yogi himself mentions their existence and that one can become involved with them.[31] He sees little harm in them however, except that one can gain only a small amount of power from them, whereas in meditating and contacting Being, the power is unlimited.

The danger here is that these spirits can harm a human being, and this has been experienced by some in TM. The Maharishi fails to see this, nor does he understand the dangers because of his interpretation of spirits as a part of Being. Many people try to rationalize this problem away. The Bible states that there are demons — created spirit beings which follow Satan and oppose God and which can make havoc among mankind. The Bible offers an answer to man's dilemma with demons — Jesus Christ as Savior and Lord. Transcendental Meditation offers none.

Though the above does not exhaust the problem areas which can and have occurred in transcendental meditation, it does provide us with a basis for concluding that there definitely are some dangers inherent in the practice of TM. Transcendental meditation has provided some benefits for some who have practiced it, and because of this, the dangers have evidently been minimized and/or overlooked.

The dangers inherent in transcendental meditation and the evidence which indicates that the practice of TM is not as unique nor as great as claimed seems to demand the verdict that transcendental meditation cannot be the best thing for a person to practice. That people feel better or, at least, think that they feel better does not necessarily mean that they were actually made better through the practice of TM. It also indicates that the Maharishi's doctrine or understanding of person as set forth in the last chapter is not the true understanding of what person is. If it were, then the dangers inherent in the practice of TM would not be present. In this light, then, the beneficial aspects of transcendental meditation would be understood as one or more of the alternative interpretations set forth in the last chapter.[32] Certainly it could be demonic deception, as noted above. It could also be deceptive self-hypnosis, an interpretation which the Maharishi himself indicates.[33] Or it could be Self-Deification, as Dr. Zaehner has discovered in his studies with Hinduism.[34]

Further studies and research are needed and welcomed. Yes, there are studies which indicate some benefits of transcendental meditation. But there are also those which point up grave dangers.

Thus far we have considered the effects of transcendental meditation upon the individual only. In concluding this section, we should note the effect of TM upon collective mankind, upon society. What kind of society will transcendental meditation produce in the future if it continues to grow. Will it produce world peace, life on a higher level — a utopian age? The Maharishi says we have entered the age of enlightenment. What will TM really help bring about?

The only way we can predict what the future will be like is on the basis of what has been accomplished in the past. Historically, transcendental meditation has never produced a society greater than that which you will find in India today. This is truly the highest moment of Hindu and TM history. Indian society, under the influence of the great commentator of the Hindu scriptures, Shankara, as well as under the Maharishi's teacher, Sri Guru Dev, has never generated anything better.

In India, Monism or the Science of Being as set forth by the Maharishi Mahesh Yogi is not just a philosophy or some term tossed about. There it is life. People are starving and dying because of living in TM's metaphysical world. Lack of concern for others, insulation against the feelings of others is a way of life. More attention is paid to the sacred cow than to a starving child with a bloated stomach.

This depersonalization of mankind, this despair, is one of the most shocking effects of Monism. The distinctions between God, man and animal are broken down. Thus man, his true identity lost, is dehumanized, and this action reaches out to affect the entire society.

When the Maharishi Mahesh Yogi was interviewed on the Merv Griffin television program, he was faced with the question of life in India. He smiled and replied, "Not everyone meditates." Fortunately for the poor Indians! The fact remains that TM's metaphysic has produced a fragmented society with every kind of ill in India today. It has increased rather than alleviated their problems.

Today in America, this researcher has noted some of the same results in the lives of meditators. Admittedly, the sampling is small at present; but such things as passively insulating oneself against the feeling of others, etc., are some of the effects seen in meditators. Blurring of problems rather than solving problems also is evident. One couple who had marriage problems prior to becoming meditators for four and one-half years discovered that TM did not solve their problems; it only caused them to ignore these problems while focusing on meditation. They became seekers of self-fulfillment. Is it possible that some effects of TM are very early developments of the Hindu way of life?

Transcendental meditation leaves us with no hope for the solution of man's problems and his ultimate dilemma.

Whether one examines the practical effects of TM upon the individual or upon society, when the evidence is weighed, TM is found greatly lacking in solutions for mankind.

Notes

1. *Time, op. cit.* p. 71.
2. Example: Transcendental Meditation is like "trying to explain the innards of color television set to a tribe of Pygmies. What you can do is tell the Pygmy how to switch on the set and tune in to a station so he can enjoy the program." Used by Lawrence Donash, chancellor of the Maharishi European Research University in Weggis, Switzerland.
3. For example, Jhan Robbins, *op. cit.,* p. 148.
4. See *Fundamentals of Progress,* published by the World Plan Executive Committee of the International Meditation Society, 1974.
5. *Springfield (Mass.) Republican,* March 24, 1974.
6. *New York Times,* December 11, 1972, p. 47.
7. *Ibid.*
8. As recorded in "Learning to Relax Through Transcendental Meditation," *Family Circle,* July 1974, p. 50.
9. As recorded in "Project Blocked," *New Jersey Herald,* August 14, 1974, p. 1.
10. *Time, op. cit.,* p. 73.
11. *Ibid.*
12. Leon S. Otis, "The Facts on Transcendental Meditation Part III," *Psychology Today,* April 1974, p. 45.

13. Robbins, *op. cit.,* p. 148.

14. Herbert Benson, *The Relaxation Response,* p. 83.

15. Otis, *op. cit.;* cf McMillan, *op. cit.,* p. 2.

16. Paul H. Levine, "Transcendental Meditation and the Science of Creative Intelligence." *Phi Delta Kappa,* December 1972, p. 232.

17. "Introduction," *Fundamentals of Progress,* published by the World Plan Executive Committee of the International Meditation Society.

18. Una Kroll, *The Healing Potential of Transcendental Meditation,* p. 66.

19. Benson, *op. cit.,* p. 79ff.; cf. "Mind Over Drugs," *Time,* October 25, 1971, p. 51.

20. Gary Schwartz, "The Facts About Transcendental Meditation Part II," *Psychology Today,* April 1974, pp. 39-44.

21. Benson, *op. cit.,* pp. 45-6.

22. As recorded in *Time,* October 13, 1974, p. 74.

23. William Johnston, *Silent Music,* p. 92.

24. Kroll, *op. cit.,* p. 169.

25. *London Times,* June 30, 1972.

26. Kroll, *op. cit.,* p. 159.

27. McMillan, *op. cit.,* p. 2; cf. Otis, *op. cit.,* p. 46.

28. Kroll, *op. cit.,* p. 169.

29. From a condensation of Barbara B. Brown's book *New Mind, New Body: Biofeedback: New Directions for the Mind,* as found in *Psychology Today,* August 1974, p. 106.

30. As recorded in the *National Courier,* November 5, 1975, p. 24.

31. Maharishi Mahesh Yogi, *Transcendental Meditation: Serenity Without Drugs,* p. 97ff.

32. See Gordon R. Lewis, *What Everyone Should Know About Transcendental Meditation;* see chapter 7.

33. Maharishi Mahesh Yogi, *op. cit.,* p. 279.

34. R. C. Zaehner, *Hindu and Muslim Mysticism,* chapter on "Self Deification."

Conclusion

Though we live in a sophisticated age in which science and technology are supposed to make life easier, they have succeeded only in intensifying the problems of daily living. Certainly they have not provided answers to the pressure, stress and anxiety of man. The number of people in our day visiting psychologists, psychiatrists and counselors is unparalleled in history. With each new generation additional stress and complexity are generated, with no real relief in sight.

How does one cope with the stresses and pressures of everyday life? If you turn on your television set and notice the advertising, you will see how we are being conditioned to respond in dealing with such problems as tension and insomnia. "Six of these...or three of these...or one of these."[1] Or, as one of the advertising jingles sings it: "Plop, plop. Fizz, fizz. Oh, what a relief it is!"[2] Simply take a tablet or a capsule and your problems will disappear!

Into these circumstances comes Transcendental Meditation, offering a solution in the form of a technique and a forty-minute-a-day practice. That it will be helpful is inevitable — it forces one to close off the mind from external thoughts, pressures and stresses, producing a mental solitude. One *should* feel better as a result of such a practice.

However, transcendental meditation is a religious solution: it is an aspect of Hinduism and operates in a Hindu metaphysic from which it derives its meaning. The Maharishi has made the claim that TM is *not* religious. He has stated TM is simply a mental technique not belonging to any one metaphysical system. One can find these statements in his writings, and yet also in the very same writings are found statements that lead us to conclude that TM *is* religious — that it leads to what the Maharishi calls "God-realization" and that it operates in a Hindu metaphysical system. How can he write that TM can lead to the God-realized life here on earth and then state in the same books, as well as in lecture, that it is not religious? In other words, how can TM be religious and not religious at the same time?

The answer to this apparent contradiction lies in the radically different way of thinking and reasoning in the East compared to that of the West. In America we have been raised in the context of Aristotelian logic in which we derive conclusions from premises by using certain laws of reasoning. One of these laws is that of non-contradiction, i.e., that one cannot hold both A and non-A to be true at the same time. Something cannot be both black and white at the same time, nor can something be religious and not religious at the same time.

In the East one does not reason by the same laws of logic as one does in the West. Thus the Maharishi, like other gurus and Indian philosophers, can be paradoxical, believing and teaching contradictory things without concern. The law of noncontradiction is not even considered by the East. So it matters little that one knows transcendental meditation is a religious technique and yet teaches it as a mental technique, denying it is religious. To demonstrate the practical outworking of this reasoning, consider the following statement from the writings of the Maharishi: "Not in the name of God-realization can we call a man to meditate in the world today, but in the name of enjoying the world better, sleeping well at night, being wide awake during the day." [3] Describe it by whatever terms you choose and it is still "God-realization."

Not only is transcendental meditation a religious technique, an aspect of Hinduism, but we have seen that there is very good reason to conclude that TM is not unique, nor is it good for mankind to practice, having some inherent dangers. TM is not *the* answer, nor the best answer, nor *any* answer to man's problem in this "pressure-cooker world."

Dr. Benson has offered a purely nonreligious technique, developed and tested at Harvard's Thorndike Memorial Laboratory, as a method of gaining relief from the pressures and stresses of life. He calls it "The Relaxation Response." This technique "was found to produce the same physiologic changes as...observed during the practice of transcendental meditation." [4]

There are several methods or techniques of relaxation available today, some which are religious and some which are not. In contrast to those above, the Bible gives an answer to the current problems of mankind. The gospel of Jesus Christ, when believed and applied to the lives of men, not only does more for the individual but it also transforms the culture to its highest level.

The power of Jesus Christ to reclaim drug addicts, homosexuals, alcoholics, and the worst of society and to recreate them in the true image of God is infinitely superior to anything that the world has to offer. Changed lives through the power of Jesus Christ is verification in the laboratory of life as to the truth of Jesus' statement: "I am come that they might have life, and that they might have it more abundantly." [5]

The power of the gospel of Jesus Christ to change society is also infinitely superior. The thrilling saga of the *Mutiny on the Bounty* has been retold and popularized in books and newspapers for years, but there is one incident of this true story that can illustrate for us the power of the Gospel upon society.

As I recall the story, mutineers sank their ship and landed on the lonely island named Pitcairn. There were nine British sailors, six Tahitian men and ten women. One of the sailors discovered a method of distilling alcohol, and the island colony soon became debauched with drunkenness and vice.

After a time, only one of the white sailors survived, surrounded by women and children. His name was Alexander Smith. He found a Bible in one of the chests taken from *The Bounty* and began to teach its principles to those who survived with him, resulting in great changes in his own life and ultimately in the lives of the entire colony. In 1808 the United States ship *Topaz* visited the island and found a thriving and prosperous community without liquor, without a jail, without crime, and without an insane asylum. The Gospel had changed the life of that entire island.

In view of the subject of this book, the importance of prayer in the Christian's life cannot be overestimated. Prayer offers spiritual benefits in answered prayer and also in the communication with God himself. But *it seems as though Christians are unaware today that prayer also has psychological benefits, removing the stresses and pressures of life, relieving stress and making you a healthier person — and with no inherent dangers.*

Jesus Christ becomes the answer to the problem of life in a "pressure-cooker world." He said: "Come unto me, all ye that labor and are heavy laden, and I will give you rest." [6] As people come into right relationship with God through Jesus Christ they find healing and life in a real world, not only for the present, but into the eternal future.

Notes

1. TV ad for Contac.
2. TV ad for Alka Seltzer.
3. Maharishi Mahesh Yogi, *Meditation of Maharishi Mahesh Yogi*, p. 168.
4. Benson, *op. cit.*, p. 87.
5. John 10:10.
6. Matthew 11:28.

Appendix A
Transcendental Meditation's Initiatory Puja
(translated from Sanskrit by a Hindu Priest)

INVOCATION

Whether pure or impure, whether purity or impurity is permeating everywhere, whoever opens himself to the expanded vision of unbounded awareness gains inner and outer purity.

INVOCATION

To *Lord Narayana,* to lotus-born *Brahma* the Creator, to *Vashishtha,* to *Shakti* and his son *Parashar.*

To *Vyasa,* to *Shukadeva,* to the great *Gaudapada,* to *Govinda,* ruler among the yogis, to his disciple.

Shri Shankaracharya, to his disciples *Padma Pada* and *Hasta Malaka* and *Trotakacharya* and *Vartika-Kara,* to others, to the tradition of our masters, I bow down.

To the abode of the wisdom of the *Shrutis, Smritis* and *Puranas,* to the abode of kindness, to the personified glory of the *Lord,* to *Shankara,* emancipator of the world, I bow down.

To *Shankaracharya* the redeemer, hailed as *Krishna* and *Badarayana,* to the commentator of the *Brahma Sutras,* I bow down.

To the glory of the *Lord* I bow down again and again, at whose door the whole galaxy of gods pray for perfection day and night.

Adorned with immeasurable glory, preceptor of the whole world, having bowed down to him we gain fulfilment.

Skilled in dispelling the cloud of ignorance of the people, the gentle emancipator, *Brahmananda Sarasvati,* the supreme teacher, full of brilliance. Him I bring to my awareness.

Offering the invocation to the lotus feet of *Shri Guru Dev,* I bow down.

Offering a seat to the lotus feet of *Shri Guru Dev,* I bow down.

Offering an ablution to the lotus feet of *Shri Guru Dev,* I bow down.

Offering cloth to the lotus feet of *Shri Guru Dev,* I bow down.

Offering sandalpaste to the lotus feet of *Shri Guru Dev,* I bow down.

Offering full rice to the lotus feet of *Shri Guru Dev,* I bow down.

Offering a flower to the lotus feet of *Shri Guru Dev,* I bow down.

Offering incense to the lotus feet of *Shri Guru*

Dev, I bow down.

Offering light to the lotus feet of *Shri Guru Dev,* I bow down.

Offering water to the lotus feet of *Shri Guru Dev,* I bow down.

Offering fruit to the lotus feet of *Shri Guru Dev,* I bow down.

Offering a betel leaf to the lotus feet of *Shri Guru Dev,* I bow down.

Offering a coconut to the lotus feet of *Shri Guru Dev,* I bow down.

OFFERING CAMPHOR LIGHT

White as camphor, kindness incarnate, the essence of creation garlanded with *Brahman,* ever dwelling in the lotus of my heart, the creative impulse of cosmic life, to That, in the form of *Guru Dev,* I bow down.

Offering light to the lotus feet of *Shri Guru Dev,* I bow down.

Offering water to the lotus feet of *Shri Guru Dev,* I bow down.

OFFERING A HANDFUL OF FLOWERS

Guru in the glory of *Brahma, Guru* in the glory of *Vishnu, Guru* in the glory of the great *Lord Shiva, Guru* in the glory of the personified transcendental fulness of *Brahman,* to Him, to *Shri Guru Dev* adorned with glory, I bow down. The Unbounded, like the endless canoply of the sky, the omnipresent in all creation, by whom the sign of That has been revealed to Him, to *Shri Guru Dev*, I bow down.

Guru Dev, Shri Brahmananda, bliss of the Absolute, transcendental joy, the Self-Sufficient, the embodiment of pure knowledge which is beyond and above the universe like the sky, the aim of "Thou art That" and other such expressions which unfold eternal Truth, the One, the Eternal, the Pure, the Immovable, the Witness of all intellects, whose status transcends thought, the Transcendent along with the three gunas, the true preceptor, to *Shri Guru Dev*, I bow down. The blinding darkness of ignorance has been removed by applying the balm of knowledge. The eye of knowledge has been opened by Him and therefore, to Him, to *Shri Guru Dev*, I bow down.

Offering a handful of flowers to the lotus feet of *Shri Guru Dev, I bow down.*

Appendix B
The Bible vs. the Maharishi's Interpretation of the Bible

Hinduism, like others of the Eastern religions, teaches that because of imperfect senses and lack of divine consciousness, characteristic of every person, the scriptures are best interpreted through a perfectly realized medium or teacher who alone can give the "pure interpretation." Just as professors and textbooks are necessary in learning, so also the guru and the scriptures are necessary for learning spiritual truth.

In the case of transcendental meditation, it becomes the Maharishi Mahesh Yogi's interpretation of the scriptures, including the Bible,[1] which is truth. Anyone who doubts this can merely note how TM instructors mimic and use the Maharishi's interpretation in the examples from the Bible which they use.[2]

The question before us is whether or not his interpretation is correct. To do this we will consider some passages as interpreted by the Maharishi and used by TM instructors and examine these to see if the Bible is actually saying this.

(1) "The kingdom of heaven is within you" (Luke 17:21). The Maharishi contends that Jesus Christ, by these words, taught that the kingdom of heaven can be found within oneself and that is where man must look for it.[3]

Perhaps the best interpretation and understanding of these words spoken by our Lord is, "The kingdom of heaven is *among* you" — that the kingdom has already arrived and is among the believers in Christ. This is in perfect harmony with the totality of Jesus' teaching on the kingdom which can be summarized by saying: Jesus taught that the kingdom of heaven is already a present reality in Him, but that its final consummation lies in the future when Jesus comes in divine majesty. Thus the Maharishi's interpretation is wrong.

In contrast to the Maharishi's teaching, Jesus taught that within man was not the kingdom of heaven or the good, but evil. In Mark 7:21-23 we read these words spoken by Jesus: "For from within, out of the heart of man, come evil thoughts, fornication, theft, murder, adultery, coveting, wickedness, deceit, licentiousness, envy, slander, pride, foolishness. All these evil things come from within, and they defile a man."

(2) "Be still and know that I am God" (Ps. 46:10). The Maharishi interprets this: "Be still and know that you are God, and when you know that you are God you will begin to live God-hood."[4]

First of all, the Maharishi incorrectly ascribes this saying to Christ.[5] It appears only in the Psalms. Secondly, you will notice his erroneous restatement from "I am God" to "you are God."

These words in context are addressed to the discomfited foes of God and His people, calling upon them to desist from their attacks and recognize the existence and greatness of the personal Creator God. Thus the teaching of the Maharishi that man is divine is not the statement of this passage nor is it the teaching of the Bible.

(3) "It is written, that the Christ should suffer..." (Luke 24:46). In this case the Maharishi denies this. He states, "I don't think that Christ ever suffered or that Christ could have suffered."[6] And again, "The message of Christ has never been that of suffering."[7]

Surely the Maharishi is wrong here. The Old Testament prophecies speak of the suffering Servant who was to come. Isaiah 53 bears witness of this. Jesus, before ascending on high, opened the minds of His disciples to the understanding of the scripture: "Thus it is written, that the Christ should suffer...You are witnesses of these things" (Luke 24:46-8). The New Testament and history as well tell us that Christ suffered; He suffered in the garden, He suffered in the scourging, and He suffered in His crucifixion.

Suffering is a part of the real world in which we live, and Jesus presented a way of victory in the face of suffering, not an escape from it. He lived in the midst of it. The secret of His triumph was His identification with the will of the Father in heaven. It was through His death on the cross that He paid the price for our sins, and in our trusting Him for salvation and living before Him and with Him we too can have victory over the sufferings of this world. It is in Him that one day all suffering will cease (Rev. 21:4).

(4) "Like a tree planted by streams of waters" (Ps. 1:3).

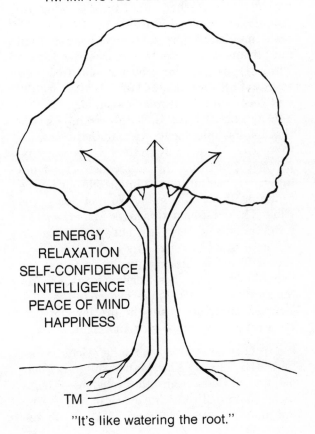

TM IMPROVES ALL AREAS OF LIFE

ENERGY
RELAXATION
SELF-CONFIDENCE
INTELLIGENCE
PEACE OF MIND
HAPPINESS

TM

"It's like watering the root."

The preceding diagram illustrates the Maharishi's interpretation of Psalm 1.[8] The life, health and growth of a tree is dependent upon the sustenance — food and water — which it takes in through its roots. Without proper food and water, a tree has difficulty in growing, remaining healthy and bearing fruit. So it is also with man, according to the Maharishi. Man must transcend his outer being and meditate within, thus drawing nourishment from the source of all existence, or Being.[9] To be healthy and "bear fruit," one must meditate.

Going back to the Bible, it certainly is true that the Psalmist likens the man that is blessed to a tree planted by waters. However, the passage states that this blessedness is not obtained by meditating within oneself but by the centering of one's life in the Word of God — the Bible. The question here is in the Maharishi's interpretation and the Christian's interpretation of the phrase "by water." Is it Being or God's Word? The Psalmist specifically says that the blessed man is one whose "delight is in the law of the Lord (i.e., the written revelation of His will). Verse 2 continues, "and in his law he [the blessed man] meditates day and night."

(5)"Thou shalt have no other Gods before me" (Ex. 20:3). The Maharishi's theology defines the Gods of all other religions as being the same in reality: Being, or Brahman of Hinduism. Writes the Maharishi: "All attributes, qualities and features belong on the relative field of life, whereas the impersonal God is of an absolute nature...impersonal, and attributeless, but it is the source of all relative existence." [10] In other words, your God may be a personal God on this level of life, but in reality He is the impersonal Being of the Maharishi's metaphysic. Thus the eternal personal God of the Bible, who created everything that exists out of nothing and not by emanations from His Being, has become merely one way of looking at Being.

Actually, the Bible says this personal Creator God exists and that He alone is God. Any other concept, including Brahman or Being, is to be rejected as "false gods" — and that is the Bible's understanding of Exodus 20:3 as seen throughout its entirety.

(6) "I am the way, the truth and the life. No man cometh to the father but by me" (John 14:6). The Maharishi denies this claim of Jesus, making transcendental meditation "the only way to salvation and success in life: there is no other way." [11]

The Bible specifically says that Jesus Christ is the only way to God. In Acts 4:12 we read, "There is none other name under heaven given among men, whereby we must be saved." As noted above, the Lord Jesus Christ himself taught this. If Jesus Christ is who He claims to be, God Incarnate, then we have the authoritative word of God himself on the subject. If He is

God and there is no other Savior, then obviously He is the only way to God.

As pointed out in the section on "The Metaphysical Question," Christian theology as set forth in the Bible is totally incompatible with that of Transcendental Meditation and Hinduism as set forth by the Maharishi Mahesh Yogi. The Bible cannot be interpreted in a Hindu metaphysic such as TM and still maintain the same meaning to the Christian. TM results in reinterpretation or denial — exactly as we have seen in this section.

MORAL: Don't be fooled by the meditator's use of the Bible in support of TM.

Notes

1. Maharishi Mahesh Yogi, *Meditations of Maharishi Mahesh Yogi*, p. 63.
2. Some of these examples can be seen in Jack Forem's book, *Transcendental Meditation.*
3. *Ibid.*
4. *Ibid.*, p. 178.
5. *Ibid.*
6. *Ibid.*, p. 123.
7. *Ibid.*, p. 89.
8. As diagrammed in a free lecture on TM by an instructor.
9. Examples of this appear in the Maharishi's writings, *e.g., Transcendental Meditation: Serenity Without Drugs*, pp. 86, 106; etc.
10. *Ibid.*, pp. 265-6.
11. Maharishi Mahesh Yogi, *On the Bhagavad-Gita*, p. 228.

Appendix C
"The Metamorphosis of TM — from Religious to Secular"

There are several areas, historically, which demonstrate the transformation of Transcendental Meditation from the religious to the secular. 1967-1968 seems to be the year of change, and this can be seen by the resultant change in the presentation of TM, in the apparent change in the mantras from those used before this period (Râma, compound forms of AUM, etc. which indicated clear Hindu participation) as distinct from those after (Kirīm, Shīrīm, Hīrīm, etc.), and most noteably in the change in the purposes of their organizational structures.

The original organization to promulgate the teachings of Maharishi Mahesh Yogi here in America — The Spiritual Regeneration Movement Foundation — was founded in 1959 in the State of California in which it was incorporated.

An amended Certificate of Incorporation filed in 1961 sets forth the basic purpose of this group as follows:

> *The corporation is a religious one;* the educational purpose shall be to give instruction in a system of meditation, and the charitable nature of the corporation is to provide a means of such instruction to *worthy persons sincerely desirous of leading a more spiritual life....* (from *Article Eleventh*)

By 1967 the Spiritual Regeneration Movement had not attracted many followers, and so a self-evaluation was instituted. In September of that year, the beginnings of the present conglomerate of organizations was started with the filing of the Certificate of Incorporation for the Students International Meditation Society (SIMS). The purpose of this organization is stated in Article II:

> The primary purpose and object of this corporation is to teach and advance a *spiritual transcendental system of meditation. The spiritual leader and teacher is Maharishi Mahesh Yogi....*

By 1968 the re-evaluation of TM was completed and a metamorphosis begun. In June of that year, SIMS amended their Certificate of Incorporation in accord with this change. Article II now read:

The primary purpose of this corporation is teaching the principle and practice of transcendental meditation. The founder or his successors shall appoint all teachers....

From this point on TM was no longer to be considered religious or spiritual, but a simple mental technique of science or life. As the Maharishi himself states: "Not in the name of God-realization can we call a man to meditate in the world today, but..." —and that is exactly the transformation of TM from the religious to the secular.

Bibliography

Herbert Benson, *The Relaxation Response,* New York: William Morrow, Inc., 1975.

Harold Bloomfield, Michael Peter Cain; Dennis Jaffe, *TM: Discovering Inner Energy and Overcoming Stress,* New York: Delacorte, 1975.

Anthony Campbell, *Seven Stages of Consciousness,* New York: Harper & Row, 1974.

Denise Denniston, Peter McWilliams, Barry Geller, *The TM Book,* New York: Price/Stern/Sloan-Versemonger, 1974.

Martin Ebon (Ed.), *Maharishi, the Guru,* New York: New American Library, 1968.

David Fisher and Jhan Robbins, *Tranquility Without Pills: All About Transcendental Meditation,* New York: Bantam Books, 1972.

Jack Forem, *Transcendental Meditation,* New York E. P. Dutton & Co., 1974.

William Gibson, *A Season in Heaven,* New York: Bantam Books, 1975.

Os Guinness, *The East, No Exit,* Downers Grove, Ill.: InterVarsity Press, 1974.

Patricia Drake Hemingway, *The Transcendental Meditation Primer,* New York: David McKay Co. Inc., 1974.

William Johnston, *Silent Music: The Source of Meditation,* New York: Harper & Row, 1974.

Una Kroll, *The Healing Potential of Transcendental Meditation,* Atlanta, Ga.: John Knox Press, 1975.

Gordon R. Lewis, *What Everyone Should Know About Transcendental Meditation,* Glendale, Calif.: Gospel Light Publishers, 1975.

Og Mandino, *The Greatest Salesman in the World,* New York: Bantam Books, 1975.

C. Naranjo and R. E. Ornstein, *On the Psychology of Meditation,* New York: Viking Press, 1971.

Helena Olson, *A Hermit in the House,* London: SRM, 1974.

T. W. Organ, *The Hindu Quest for the Perfection of Man,* Athens, Ohio: Ohio University Press, 1970.

Douglas Shah, *The Meditators,* Plainfield, N.J.: Logos International, 1975.

Adam Smith, *Powers of Mind,* New York: Random House, 1975.

John White, *Everything You Want To Know About TM,* New York: Pocket Books, 1976.

Maharishi Mahesh Yogi, *Meditations of Maharishi Mahesh Yogi,* New York: Bantam Books, 1968.

Maharishi Mahesh Yogi, *On the Bhagavad-Gita,* Baltimore, Md.: Penguin Books, 1967.

Maharishi Mahesh Yogi, *The Science of Being and Art of Living,* London: SRM, 1966.

Maharishi Mahesh Yogi, *Transcendental Meditation: Serenity Without Drugs,* New York: New American Library, 1963.

R. C. Zaehner, *Hindu and Muslim Mysticism,* New York: Schoeken Books, 1960.